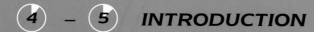

CONTENTS

4 – 5 **INTRODUCTION**

6 – 7 **SUPERBIKES**

8 – 9 **WORLD SUPERBIKES**

10 – 11 **DIRT BIKES**

12 – 13 **MOTOCROSS**

14 – 15 **DRAGSTERS**

16 – 17 **SPEEDWAY**

18 – 19 **ICE SPEEDWAY**

20 – 21 **CUSTOM BIKES**

22 – 23 **MINIMOTOS**

24 – 25 **SIDECAR RACING**

26 – 27 **DESERT RACERS**

28 – 29 **LAND SPEED BIKES**

30 **USEFUL CONTACTS**

31 **TECHNICAL TERMS**

32 **INDEX**

INTRODUCTION

Ever wanted to know what it feels like to ride some of the most powerful motorbikes in the world? Then The Need for Speed will show you.

This book takes a look at an amazing range of bikes – and some of the ridiculous things people do with them. Take part in the fiercely competitive world of superbike racing. Blast your way around a dirt track on a thundering Harley-Davidson. Or venture out into a hot, dusty desert on a gruelling 14,484-km (9000-mile) course as you compete to find out just how tough you and your bike are.

As well as the thrills and spills, we also give you the facts and figures behind these incredible machines. For most types of motorcycle featured there is a Stat File and a Fact File.

This line tells you which type and model of motorcycle is being looked at.

These lines give details about such things as engine size, power and top speed.

The technical terms used in this book are explained on page 31.

STAT FILE

World Superbike

Engine type	Honda four-stroke
Engine size	750cc
Power	150bhp
Number of cylinders	4
Top speed	290km/h (180mph)
Acceleration	0–100km/h in 2.9 seconds

The need for
SPEED
Motorbikes

4

Written by Philip Raby & Simon Nix

W
FRANKLIN WATTS
LONDON · SYDNEY

CREDITS

This edition published in 2000 by Franklin Watts
96 Leonard Street
London EC2A 4XD

Franklin Watts Australia
14 Mars Road
Lane Cove
NSW 2066

© Franklin Watts 1999

Text: Philip Raby and Simon Nix
Series editor: Mathew Parselle
Designed by: Perry Associates
Art director: Robert Walster

A CIP catalogue record for this book
is available from the British Library

ISBN 0 7496 3161 9 (Hb)
       0 7496 3917 2 (Pb)
Dewey Decimal Classification 796.7

Printed in Dubai

Picture credits: Cover: Front middle and back inset –
Martin Grosse-Geldermann; front bottom – Allsport/Stu
Forster; back – Ray Archer Photography
Superbikes – Suzuki UK; Kawasaki UK; Yamaha UK;
Honda UK; World superbikes – Kawasaki UK; Honda UK;
Suzuki UK/James Whitham/Peter Goddard; Gold and
Goose; Dirt bikes – Mac McDiarmid; Motocross –
Kawasaki UK; Ray Archer; Yamaha UK; Dragsters –
Martin Grosse-Geldermann; Speedway – Allsport/ Anton
Want/Stu Forster; Ice speedway – Allsport/Mike
Hewitt/Chris Cole/Bob Martin/Clive Brunskill; Custom
bikes – Gold and Goose; Double Red/James Wright;
Quadrant Photo Library; Minimotos – Allsport/Gary M.
Prior/Clive Mason; Sidecar racing – Allsport/Mike
Cooper; Quadrant Photo Library/Ken McKay; Desert
racers – BMW; Land speed bikes – Quadrant Photo
Library/Roland Brown

The Fact File gives a slightly unusual, strange or funny bit of information about the bike.

FACT FILE

There are lots of different tyres for World Superbikes, to suit the weather conditions. Some tyres have softer rubber on the edges than the middle to help them grip as the bike goes around corners.

SUPERBIKES

Superbikes are the most powerful type of road-going motorcycle. They speed along faster than some of the most expensive sports cars, yet they cost a fraction of the price.

Superbikes look like racing bikes (see pages 8-9), but are made to be ridden on the road. Some can travel at speeds of up to 306km/h (190mph) – and they take corners superbly.

Superbikes can accelerate from 0-100km/h (0-60mph) in an impressive three seconds or less. What's more, they can nip in and out of traffic, which means that long distances can be travelled quickly and easily.

STAT FILE

Production Superbike

Engine type	Kawasaki four-stroke
Engine size	900cc
Power	127bhp
Number of cylinders	4
Top speed	274km/h (170mph)
Acceleration	0-100km/h in 3 seconds

FACT FILE

The R1's 1000cc four-cylinder engine produces over 140bhp. All this power is transferred to the road by the back wheel. This means that the back tyre wears out very quickly. It has to be replaced about every 2414km (1500 miles).

Superbikes corner well because they have a low centre of gravity, which means that the weight of the engine is low down near the road. The rider sits very low, too. On some superbikes, the rider almost lies flat on his stomach with his feet behind him and his arms in front. This make the bike more streamlined – it cuts through the air easily. The streamlining is also helped by a fairing – a plastic screen on the front of the bike over which the air flows.

Yamaha YZF1000 R1

One of the most exciting superbikes is the Japanese Yamaha YZF1000R1. This costs less than a small family car, but has pushed the boundaries of out-and-out performance to new limits. Only the very best motorcyclists can safely handle such powerful machines. Superbikes are also made by other Japanese companies, such as Honda and Kawasaki, as well as the Italian Ducati firm.

Honda CBR 1000 Blackbird

WORLD SUPERBIKES

The ultimate motorcycle racing takes place on racetracks but uses bikes similar to ones you can ride on the road.

World Superbike racing has taken over from Grand Prix racing as the most popular racing spectacle. This is because Grand Prix bikes are specially built machines, whereas World Superbikes are based on fast road bikes, which the spectators can buy themselves.

World Superbike racing began in 1988. The rules say that the machines must look like, and be derived from, road bikes. This keeps the costs down and also leads to fierce competition on the racetrack.

There are two basic types of bike that compete: the 750cc four cylinder racers and the twin cylinder 1000cc machines.

Superbike racing is especially popular in Britain and the USA as there always lots of riders from these countries involved.

Knee Slide

STAT FILE

World Superbike

Engine type	Honda four-stroke
Engine size	750cc
Power	150bhp
Number of cylinders	4
Top speed	290km/h (180mph)
Acceleration	0-100km/h in 2.9 seconds

FACT FILE

There are lots of different tyres for World Superbikes, to suit the weather conditions. Some tyres have softer rubber on the edges than the middle to help them grip as the bike goes around corners.

Burning leather

The top-class circuit racers lean their bikes over so far when they are swooping around fast bends that they have to wear special knee sliders that scrape the ground. These are made from either hard plastic or leather and are attached by Velcro straps. This way, as soon as the sliders are worn out they can be easily replaced. There are smaller versions on the sides of their boots.

DIRT BIKES

Imagine a giant version of speedway racing with a larger track and bigger, more powerful bikes. That's dirt-bike racing – a sport that thrills American audiences.

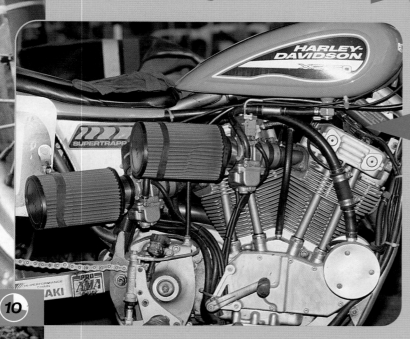

Dirt-bike racing started off as being very similar to speedway events, but soon moved on and became a sport in its own right.

In the 1920s, dirt bikes sped around horse-racing tracks, which had loose, dusty surfaces.

By the 1950s, the sport had developed into America's most popular form of motorcycle racing and special tracks were built. These were big mile-long ovals with jumps built in, just to make the sport even more exciting.

Riders pitch their bikes into the sweeping corners at the ends of the oval track at speeds of 160km/h (100mph), with both wheels sliding sideways. They slide one foot along the ground to stop them falling over.

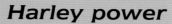

Harley power

Modern dirt bikes are specially built for the sport. One of the favourites among riders is the Harley-Davidson. This uses a thundering 750cc V-twin engine. The big engine produces about 90bhp, which means that the bikes have a top speed of over 209km/h (130mph).

STAT FILE

Dirt Bike

Engine type	Harley Davidson four-stroke
Engine size	750cc
Power	70bhp
Number of cylinders	V2
Top speed	193km/h (120mph)
Acceleration	0-100km/h in 4.7 seconds

FACT FILE

Some dirt bikes do not have a front brake because the riders do not want to slow down as they race each other round and round.

MOTOCROSS

Some motorcycles are specially made to ride at high speed on rough dirt and mud tracks. They race in an exciting sport called motocross.

Motocross bikes are strong but lightweight. They are very tall so that the engine and frame do not hit the ground when they go over rough surfaces. The seat is normally one metre (three feet) from the ground – high compared with normal motorcycles.

There are different classes of motocross racing, with engine sizes ranging from 125cc to 500cc.

Motocross tracks have a lot of difficult obstacles for the riders to overcome. The most spectacular parts of the tracks are sharp hills, which the bikes go up at high speed and then leap off the top. This can result in riders falling off their bikes as they land.

Some motocross circuits are in big indoor arenas. The tracks are lit by floodlights so that the spectators can see the action. These indoor races are sometimes shown on television.

STAT FILE

Motocross Bike

Engine type	Honda two-stroke
Engine size	500cc
Power	65bhp
Number of cylinders	1
Top speed	129km/h (80mph)
Acceleration	0-100km/h in 4.5 seconds

FACT FILE

Motocross used to be called scrambling. You may still hear people talk about scramble bikes.

Safety gear

Motocross is a very exciting sport, but it can also be dangerous. Riders wear special clothing to reduce the chance of being injured if they fall off.

As well as a crash helmet with a visor to keep dirt out of their eyes, riders wear body armour, knee protectors, armoured gloves and steel-reinforced boots.

DRAGSTERS

A dragster is a very fast motorcycle that is specially made to run at high speeds in a straight line. Some can reach speeds of over 322km/h (200mph).

The fastest dragsters, known as top-fuel dragsters, look very different to other racing bikes. They are very long with two or even three powerful engines bolted to them.

Each engine may be up to 1400cc in size and is powered by a special, and highly expensive, fuel called nitromethane.

Drag bikes have huge back tyres called slicks because they are completely smooth. To make the back tyre grip the track as the bike accelerates, the rider warms it up before the race by spinning it. This turns the surface of the tyre into sticky molten rubber with clouds of smoke pouring from it.

The front tyre is smaller and may lift off the ground as the bike accelerates. This is called a wheelie.

Drag bikes have two tiny wheels sticking out of the back on a metal strut. This is called a wheelie bar. It stops the front wheel from lifting up too far when accelerating hard.

Because drag bikes accelerate so fast, the drivers have to lay flat on their fronts to avoid being thrown off. They have their arms stretched out in front of them, clinging onto the handlebars, and their legs behind them.

STAT FILE

Top-fuel Dragster

Engine type	Kawasaki super charged
Engine size	1400cc
Power	350bhp
Number of cylinders	4
Top speed	over 322km/h (200mph)
Acceleration	0-100km/h in 2.5 seconds

Drag strip

Drag bikes are designed to race in a straight line: they cannot turn corners. They run down a long straight track called a drag strip.

Drag strips are always 400m (1320ft) long. Some very powerful bikes can run this distance in under six seconds, which means that they are travelling at about 330km/h (205mph).

The bikes race in pairs along the drag strip. The riders are told when to start racing by a tower of coloured lights – rather like traffic lights. This is called a "Christmas tree".

SPEEDWAY

Speedway is one of the most basic but also one of the most exciting motorcycle sports. It involves tearing around a dusty track at high speed on stripped-down bikes.

The specially built machines have no brakes, no gears, simple suspension systems and can only race round the oval-shaped track in an anticlockwise direction.

This is because the riders slide sideways around the corners and there is a solid footrest mounted low down on the right-hand side of the bike: this would hit the ground if they tried to turn a clockwise corner.

Riders balance their thrilling slides by adjusting the throttle and sliding their left foot along the ground as they turn.

The bikes have big single-cylinder engines that run on a special fuel called methanol. This is very explosive but it is used because it makes the engines run very fast.

Four bikes race against each other for four laps of the circuit, either in an indoor floodlit stadium or an outdoor track.

Speedway began in America almost 100 years ago and soon became popular in Australia. The sport came to Europe in the 1920s.

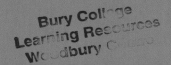

Speedway Bike

Engine type	GM four-stroke
Engine size	500cc
Power	60bhp
Number of cylinders	1
Top speed	130km/h (80mph)
Acceleration	0-100km/h in 4.5 seconds

Speed demons

Some speedway bikes use 50-horsepower 500cc engines made by a company called Weslake. Because there is no gearbox, riders can change the size of the rear sprocket before the start of the race to give either a high top speed of over 130km/h (80mph), or to give increased acceleration away from the starting tape.

FACT FILE

Speedway riders strap a thick steel plate to the bottom of their left boot to stop it wearing away or even bursting into flames as they rub it along the ground.

ICE SPEEDWAY

If you think that speedway riders are amazing on a dirt track, you should see them run on ice!

The tracks are oval shaped, just like in normal speedway, but the surface is frozen – which makes an already dangerous sport even more extreme.

When the riders are travelling very fast around bends they lean over so far that their left hand almost touches the cold surface.

The bikes are similar to those used in normal speedway. But if you tried to race on ice with conventional rubber tyres, you would slide all over the place and probably create a huge pile-up.

To avoid this, ice speedway bikes use tyres with big metal spikes. These grip the ice so that the rider is able to accelerate and turn corners without falling off.

The tyres can have up to 300 fearsome-looking spikes sticking out of them. To prevent the spikes from skewering other riders, huge guards cover both the front and back wheels for safety.

Because ice speedway needs a frozen track, you can only see the sport in very cold areas of the world, such as parts of Eastern Europe and Scandinavia.

Hidden oil

The heavier a motorbike is, the slower it will travel. To save weight, ice speedway bikes have tiny petrol tanks which hold just enough fuel to complete a four-lap race. To reduce weight further, some bikes store the engine oil inside the hollow metal frame.

STAT FILE

Ice Speedway Bike

Engine type	Jawa four-stroke
Engine size	750cc
Power	70bhp
Number of cylinders	V2
Top speed	129km/h (80mph)
Acceleration	0-100km/h in 4.5 seconds

FACT FILE

Ice speedway riders cut up sections of old rubber tyres to strap to their left knee for protection as it rubs along the ice going round corners.

CUSTOM BIKES

Some motorcyclists like to stand out from the crowd. They customise their bikes to make them look different from other ones, adding special parts and decorating them with wild paint schemes.

Custom bikes are very popular in America and most are based on the famous Harley-Davidson range.

The most spectacular custom bikes are called choppers.
Choppers have very long front forks attached to a small front wheel way in front of the rider. The bikes also have a big, fat back wheel and a huge engine with a noisy exhaust pipe.

The rider sits on a large saddle with a backrest. His feet are stretched out in front of him and he grips hold of the huge handlebars, which rise as high as his face. Choppers are made to look good, not be comfortable!

Because of their shape, choppers are not good for going fast around corners. However, they are made for going down long, straight American roads, so this is not a problem.

The metal parts of a chopper are often chrome plated. This is a sparkling metal finish which is highly polished.

20

Spray art

To make their machines even more outstanding, custom bike owners often have the small, tulip-shaped petrol tank beautifully painted. Special artists use a device called an airbrush to paint the images.

STAT FILE

Custom Bike

Engine type	Harley Davidson Fat Boy 4-stroke
Engine size	1340cc
Power	70bhp
Number of cylinders	V2
Top speed	177km/h (110mph)
Acceleration	0-100km/h in 5.5 seconds

FACT FILE

The word chopper was borrowed from American car customisers who chopped off parts of their cars to turn them into hot rods.

MINIMOTOS

Minimotos may look like toys, but these tiny motorcycles can carry adults at speeds of over 97km/h (60mph).

Minimotos are the world's smallest motorcycles. They are tiny enough to fit inside a large suitcase.

Some people use minimotos as a handy means of transport which they carry inside their caravan or yacht.

They are very easy for adults and children to ride because they have an automatic clutch and no gearbox. The only controls are a throttle to make the bike move and a brake lever to stop it. Anyone from seven years old up can ride a minimoto.

The bikes look like tiny racing motorbikes, complete with a little streamlined fairing, and they are often used for racing. The miniature machines compete in both national and international events held on karting tracks.

Chubby little racing tyres are specially produced for the sport with four grades of stickiness. They measure 10cm (4in) in diameter by 7.5cm (3in) wide.

Minimoto racing started in Japan in the 1970s, using engines from grass trimmers. The sport was refined in Italy and came to Britain and the USA in the 1990s.

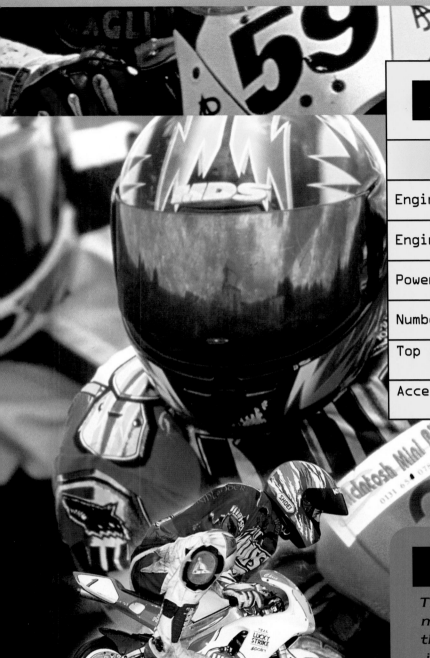

STAT FILE

Minimoto

Engine type	Two-stroke
Engine size	40cc
Power	10bhp
Number of cylinders	1
Top speed	97km/h (60mph)
Acceleration	0-100km/h in 14 seconds

FACT FILE

There is even a sidecar version of minimoto racing. Two people ride the specially built 80cc machines, just like the big sidecar bikes on pages 24-25.

Racing classes

There are three racing classes in the UK: Junior, for 7 to 13-year olds with 40cc engines producing 4bhp; Senior for 13-year olds and above with 40cc engines producing 6bhp; and Superclass for more powerful 40cc engines producing 10bhp.

SIDECAR RACING

Most racing motorcycles carry one person. However, there is a special type of racing which involves bikes with a second person sitting to the side of the driver. This is called sidecar racing.

You may think that the passenger in the sidecar would have little to do, but you'd be wrong. The passenger has a very important and difficult job. He has to move his weight around to help with handling.

When the bike is accelerating, the passenger must put all his weight over the rear wheel to push it against the ground. This makes it grip the track better.

As the bike goes around corners, the passenger must move from one side to the other to stop the machine from flipping over. Sometimes the passenger will lean right out to the side of the bike to keep it level.

A sidecar bike has a number of handgrips for the passenger to hold onto as he moves around.

The rider has a very different job to a normal bike rider. A sidecar bike is driven more like a car because it does not lean over on corners.

Because of this, the bikes do not have rounded tyres like normal motorcycles. Instead, the tyres are flat, like car tyres, so that more rubber grips the road.

STAT FILE

Sidecar Racing Bike

Engine type	Honda four-stroke
Engine size	600cc
Power	115bhp
Number of cylinders	4
Top speed	241km/h (150mph)
Acceleration	0-100km/h in 3.8 seconds

FACT FILE

Modern racing sidecar bikes are more like cars than motorcycles. Some people think that because of this they should appear at car racing events, not bike ones.

All in one

When sidecar racing started, the passenger compartment was bolted onto a normal motorcycle. Sometimes you still see motorcycles like this on the road.

Modern racing sidecar bikes are very different. Instead of a separate sidecar, the machine is built as a single unit, using technology similar to that of Formula One racing cars.

DESERT RACERS

Racing a bike through a hot, dusty desert is one of the toughest tests for both riders and their machines. The hardest courses can be up to 14,484km (9000 miles) long with the bikes covering around 800km (500 miles) a day.

Competitors usually ride big two-cylinder 750cc or 1000cc off-road motorbikes which have been specially modified to cope with the gruelling desert conditions.

Because there are very few petrol filling stations in the desert, the bikes are fitted with huge petrol tanks so that they do not run out of fuel in the middle of nowhere.

There is a lot of sand flying around in the desert. Sand will destroy a motorcycle's engine if it gets inside, so the bikes have a special air intake which stops anything harmful from entering the engine.

There are also a lot of large, hard rocks lying around. These can make holes in ordinary tyres, so the motorcycle's wheels are fitted with special thick tyres which cannot be punctured easily. What's more, the tyres are filled with foam instead of air so if one is punctured, it does not go flat.

Rocks could also fly up and hit the engine when the bike is travelling at speeds of over 160km/h (100mph), so there is a metal plate called a sump guard underneath the engine to protect it from damage.

Keeping on course

It is easy to get lost in deserts because the landscape often all looks the same. To help the rider find his way around, the motorbike has a satellite navigation system. This is an electronic device that uses information from satellites in space to tell the rider his exact location.

STAT FILE

Desert Bike

Engine type	Honda four-stroke
Engine size	600cc
Power	44bhp
Number of cylinders	1
Top speed	129km/h (80mph)
Acceleration	0-100 km/h in 5 seconds

FACT FILE

The Paris-Dakar rally is one of the hardest and longest motor-racing events. Each rider needs a back-up team to help him on the way. As well as motorcycles, cars and even lorries make the 14,484-km (9000-mile) journey from Paris in France, to Morocco in Africa, and then across the wild Sahara Desert before finishing at Dakar on the west coast of Africa. The rally was thought up by a Frenchman called Thierry Sabine back in the late 1970s.

The fastest motorbikes on earth are built specially to break the land speed record. Most motorcyclists enjoy the thrill of travelling at speed, but not many get to power along at over 483km/h (300mph).

When a bike travels very fast, it has to push the air out of the way. A normal motorcycle with a rider sitting on top of it would be slowed down. Record-breaking bikes usually have a cigar-shaped body, which encloses the rider and helps the vehicle cut through the air. This is called a cowling.

Flat out

Most race tracks have annoying corners that riders have to slow down for, and driving down public roads at such high speeds could be dangerous.

So, most record-breaking attempts are done in America on huge salt or sand flats where riders can travel at top speed for a great distance. All the motorcycle speed records since 1956 have been achieved on the Bonneville Salt Flats.

STAT FILE

UK Landspeed Record Holder

Engine type	Turbocharged Norton rotary
Engine size	588cc
Power	600bhp
Number of cylinders	none
Top speed	323.3km/h (200.9mph)
Acceleration	0-100km/h in 2.5 seconds

Record breakers

Ridden by Richard Brown (above), the Gillette Mach3 Challenger (main picture) has a rocket-shaped cowling. The motorcycle world land speed record is held by the Easyrider Streamliner. Its rider, Dave Campos, hit 518.436km/h (322.150mph) in 1990.

FACT FILE

Because riders are often fully enclosed in the long bodies of their bikes they are unable to put their feet down when the bike stops at the end of a run. Therefore, the bike is fitted with foldaway legs that deploy to stop the machine falling over.

If you want to find out more about any of the motorbikes mentioned in this book, here are some names which might be useful.

UK

British Motorcyclists Federation Limited
129 Seaforth Avenue
Motspur Park
New Malden
Surrey KT3 6JU
Tel: 0181 942 7914
Fax: 0181 949 6215
A national body for all types of motorcycling

RAC Motor Sports Association Limited
Motor Sports House
Riverside Park, Colnbrook
Slough SL3 0HG
Tel: 01753 681736
Fax: 01753 682938
The national body controlling most forms of motor sport

Silverstone Circuits Limited
Silverstone
Towcester
Northamptonshire NN12 8TN
Tel: 01327 311164
Fax: 01327 857663
The place to see World Superbikes racing

Santa Pod Raceway
Airfield Road
Hinwick
Northamptonshire
Tel: 01234 782828
Fax: 01234 782818
The home of drag racing in the UK

TECHNICAL TERMS

There are some words in this book which you may not have seen before. Here is an explanation of them.

Accelerate: drive faster.

Air intakes: holes that let air into the engine. The engine needs air to run and to keep it cool.

Automatic: a gearbox which changes gear for you.

Body armour: very strong clothing that protects the rider's body in the event of an accident.

Brakes: a mechanism inside the wheels, which makes the motorbike slow down and stop when the rider presses a foot pedal or pulls a lever on the handlebars.

Brake horsepower (bhp): see horsepower.

CC: short for cubic capacity, a measure of an engine's size. Usually, the greater the cc of an engine, the more powerful it is.

Circuit: a track that racing bikes race around.

Cylinders: compartments inside an engine where the fuel burns. Small motorbikes have a single cylinder, but more powerful ones may have two or more cylinders. If you see the letter 'V' in front of the number of cylinders, it means that there are two rows of cylinders forming a V shape. A V8 engine, for example, has two rows of four cylinders. This makes the engine shorter and stronger than a long single row of cylinders.

Crash helmet: protects the rider's head from injury in an accident.

Engine: a machine which turns the bike's rear wheel and makes it move.

Exhaust pipe: a metal pipe along which waste gases from the engine pass. Most exhaust pipes include a silencer, helping to make the motorcycle less noisy.

Frame: the metal structure to which a motorbike's engine, wheels and other parts are bolted.

Fuel: liquid that burns inside the engine to make it run. Most motorbikes run on petrol fuel.

Gears: allow the motorbike to drive fast without the engine running too fast. Most bikes have six gears. The gears are selected by a foot pedal.

Handlebars: a metal bar at the front of the motorbike, which the rider holds onto and uses to steer the machine.

Horsepower (hp): the measure of an engine's power. The higher the horsepower, the faster the motorbike. You may see horsepower written as bhp, which stands for brake horsepower.

Hot rod: A motorcycle that has been modified to make it faster and look different to a standard production model.

INDEX

acceleration 15, 17, 24; see also
    Stat Files
America 10, 16, 20, 28; see also
    USA
Australia 16

Blackbird see Honda CBR 100
Bonneville Salt Flats 28
brakes 11, 16, 22
Britain 8, 22

Campos, Dave 29,
choppers 20
"Christmas tree" 15
clothing for riders 9, 13, 17, 19
clutch 22
cowling 28

desert racing 26-27
dirt bikes 10-11
dragsters 14-15
drag strip 15
Ducati 7

Easyrider Streamliner 29
engines 7, 8, 10, 12, 14, 16, 17,
    20, 29; see also Stat Files

fairing 7, 22
frame 12
fuel 14, 16, 19, 26

gearbox 17, 22
gears 16
GM four-stroke 17
Grand Prix racing 8

handgrips 24
handlebars 15
Harley-Davidson 10, 11, 20
    Ruxton engines 29
    Fat Boy 4-stroke 21
Honda 7
    CBR 1000 Blackbird 7
    four-stroke 9, 25
    two-stroke 13

ice speedway 18-19
Italy 7, 22

Japan 22
Jawa four-stroke 19

Kawasaki 6, 7
    super charged 15

landspeed bikes 28-29

methanol 16
minimotos 22-23
    two-stroke 23
motocross 12-13

nitromethane 14
Norton Turbocharged rotary 29

off-road motorbikes 26

Paris-Dakar rally 27
passengers 24, 25
petrol tanks 19, 21, 26

race tracks 8, 10, 12, 15, 16, 18,
    22, 28
racing 8-9, 10-11, 12-13, 14-15, 16-
    17, 18-19, 22-23, 24-25, 26-27

Sabine, Thierry 27
scrambling see motocross
sidecars 23, 24-25
slicks 14
speed 6, 10, 14, 17, 22, 26, 28, 29;
    see also Stat Files
speedway 10, 16-17, 18
    ice 18-19
streamlining 7
sump guard 26
superbikes 6-7

throttle 16, 22
tyres 7, 9, 14, 18, 22, 24, 26

UK 23; see also Britain
USA 8, 22; see also America

wheelie 14
wheels 7, 10, 15, 18, 20, 24, 26
World Superbike racing 8-9

Yamaha YZF 1000 R1 7